MICHIGAN DMV

TEST MADE EASY

With over 270 Drivers test questions/Answers for Michigan DMV written Exam: 2019 Drivers Permit/License Study Book

ALGER CARR

All Rights Reserved. No Contents of this book may be reproduced in any way or by any means without a written consent of the publisher, with exception of brief excerpt in critical reviews and articles.

Study Guide

The easiest way to pass the **Michigan** driver's license test is to use this **Michigan** driving manual and our over 270 practice test questions and answers. While taking these practice exams, you will always find the correct answer therein in case you choose incorrectly so as to appraise your progress. Read the **Michigan** driver's license manual a few times and then use the practice exams as many times as you desire. We hope you will enjoy the tests. As we wish you good luck with passing your exam.

This book, split into 5 practical tests, each test consists of 65, 114, 54, 11, 46 and 14 questions respectively.

For a successful test, we strongly advise you repeat each practical test until you archive a consistent score of up to 85% and above correct answers. To navigate to specific test questions, you can use the hyperlinks on the contents page, and using the below table of content.

This practical test has over 270 test question and are an excellent way of preparing any one for the actual written test. This book contents questions for the Drivers Road Signs, Permit Practical test. Each test contains questions that are really very similar to the actual test questions. As you prepare using this practical questions bank, as opposed to reading the DMV drivers handbook which has shown to be time consuming, you will learn basic driving skills, road signs and traffic signals with their meanings. This book will among other things teach you how to answer the trick questions which always appears on the test.

Testing Strategy

Set yourself up to pass your written driver's license test with these simple tips.

• Prepare in advance weeks before the test by reading and practicing all included tests.

• Get a very good night sleep before the exam.

• Do not waste much time on hard test questions. Skip any question you do not immediately know its answers.

• Always answer or solve the easy questions first, and go back to the unanswered or hard questions letter.

• Use common sense and do not over emphasize or think on each question.

• Do not leave any question blank; always make an educated guess on each question.

• You should study the road signs test and know.

Practice Test 1

(65 Questions)

1. When you have a green light, and traffic is backed up into the intersection, what do you do in that instance?

a) Enter the intersection and hope the traffic clears before the light changes.

b) Wait until traffic clears before entering an intersection.

c) Try to go around the traffic.

d) Sound your horn to clear the intersection.

e) None of the above.

Answer: B

2. Where more than one vehicle is stopped at an intersection, which vehicle has the right-of-way?

a) The largest vehicle.

b) The first vehicle that attempts to go.

c)   The first vehicle to arrive.

d)   The vehicle on the right.

e)   None of the above.

Answer: C

3.   What is the acceptable minimum safe following distance under most conditions?

a)   A minimum of 2 seconds is the most recommended following distance under most conditions.

b)   A minimum of 4 seconds is the most recommended following distance under most conditions.

c)   A minimum of 5 seconds is the most recommended following distance under most conditions.

d)   A minimum of 6 seconds is the most recommended following distance under most conditions.

e)   None of the above.

Answer: B

4.   If you are at a highway entrance and has to wait for a gap in traffic before entering the roadway, what should you do?

a) Pull up as far as possible on the ramp and wait leaving some room behind you on the ramp for other vehicles.

b) Drive to the shoulder, wait for a gap in the roadway, then accelerate quickly.

c) Slow down on the entrance ramp as you wait for a gap, then speed up so you enter at the same speed that the traffic is moving.

d) Slow down on the entrance ramp as you wait for a gap, then sound your horn and activate your emergency flash lights to alert drivers you are entering the roadway.

e) None of the above.

Answer: C

5. When is it really ok to drive faster than the posted speed limit?

a) When being followed too closely.

b) To keep pace a with the flow of traffic.

c) If you have an emergency.

d) It is never ok.

Answer: D

6. You can cross a solid yellow line to do which of the following?

a) To make U turn on the highway.

b) To turn into a driveway when it is safe to do so.

c) To pass on the highway.

d) To get a clearer view of the road ahead.

Answer: B

7. How would you see if there is a vehicle in your blind spot?

a) Lean back and forth while looking in your mirrors.

b) Look over your shoulder.

c) Adjust the power mirrors if you have them.

d) This cannot be done, that is really why it is called a blind spot.

Answer: B

8. On a rainy, a snowy, or foggy day when it begins to get dark, and when you gradually drive away from a rising or setting sun, it is a good time to?

a) Check the tires.

b) Put on your seatbelt.

c) Turn on your headlights.

d) Roll up the windows.

e) None of the above.

Answer: C

9. Name some likely places where you may find slippery spots on the road.

a) In corners and at stop signs.

b) In shady spots as well as on overpasses and bridges.

c) In tunnels and on hills.

d) Near large bodies of water.

e) None of the above.

Answer: B

10. If you want to turn to the left at an intersection but the oncoming traffic is heavy, what would you do?

a) Wait at the crosswalk while traffic clears.

b) Wait at the center of the intersection for the traffic to clear.

c) Start your turn forcing others to stop.

d) None of the above.

Answer: B

11. What does a flashing yellow light indicate?

a) Pedestrian crossing.

b) School Crossing.

c) Stop, then proceed with caution.

d) Proceed with caution.

e) None of the above.

Answer: D

12. Whenever driving in heavy fog during the daytime you should drive with your?

a) Headlights off.

b) Parking lights on.

c) Headlights on low beam.

d) Headlights on high beam.

e) None of the above.

Answer: C

13. Which of these statements is correct?

a) A solid or dashed yellow line shows the left edge of traffic lanes going in your direction.

b) A solid or dashed yellow line shows the right edge of traffic lanes going in your direction.

Answer: A

14. After drinking alcohol, a cold shower or coffee will lower your blood alcohol content.

a) True

b) False

Answer: B

15. Put the following signs in their proper order from left to right.

a) Yield, school zone, construction.

b) School zone, construction, no passing.

c) Pass with care, construction, yield.

d) No passing, slow moving vehicle, yield.

e)   No passing, construction, yield.

Answer: D

16.   There are some situations when it is legal to double park.park.

a)   True

b)   False

Answer: B

17.   Safety belts would help you keep control of your car.

a)   True

b)   False

Answer: A

18.   What would you do if you are at an intersection and you hear a siren?

a)   Stop and do not move until after the emergency vehicle has passed.

b)   Continue through the intersection, and pull over to the right side of the road then, stop.

c)   Back pull over to the right side of the road then stop.

d)   None of the above.

Answer: B

19. The state examiner would check the person's vehicle before beginning the driving test to:

a)   Ensure the vehicle has all the necessary equipment.

b)   Make sure that the vehicle is in a safe operating condition.

c)   Check for cleanliness.

d)   A and C.

e)   A and B.

Answer: E

20. Passing is permissible in either direction if there are two solid yellow lines in the center of the road when?

a)   When following a slow truck.

b)   Only when it is safe.

c)   On US highways only.

d)   Passing is never permitted.

Answer: D

21. A driver turning left at an intersection is expected to yield to what?

a) Vehicles approaching from the opposite direction.

b) Pedestrians, bicycles and vehicles, approaching from the opposite direction.

c) Pedestrians, bicycles and vehicles, approaching from the right.

d) Pedestrians, bicycles and vehicles, approaching from the left.

e) None of the above.

Answer: B

22. What does a yellow sign indicate?

a) State highway ahead.

b) A special situation or a hazard ahead.

c) Construction work ahead.

d) Interstate Sign.

e) None of the above.

Answer: B

23. One of the basic things to remember about driving at night or in fog is to?

a) Be ready to brake more quickly.

b) Watch for cars at intersections.

c) Drive within the range of your headlights.

d) Use your high beams at all times.

e) None of the above.

Answer: C

24. When you are driving faster than other traffic on a freeway, which lane should you use?

a) The right lane.

b) The shoulder.

c) The left lane.

d) The carpool lane.

e) None of the above.

Answer: C

25. How far ahead can you look when you are on the highway?

a) 3 to 5 seconds.

b) 5 to 10 seconds.

c)   10 to 15 seconds.

d)   15 to 20 seconds.

e)   None of the above.

Answer: C

26.   A white square or a rectangular signs with white, red, or black letters or symbols are usually what kind of signs?

a)   Destination

b)   Service

c)   Route

d)   Reference

e)   Regulatory

f)   Warning

Answer : B

27.   Whenever you see a stopped vehicle on the side of the road what should you do?

a)   Stop and offer assistance.

b)   Slow down and use caution when passing.

c) Sound your horn to inform them know you are about to pass.

d) Notify emergency services.

e) None of the above.

Answer: B

28. When is it really illegal to turn right at a red light?

a) It is always legal.

b) It is not legal to turn right at a red light.

c) Only on one-way roads.

d) Only if there is a no-turn-on-red signposted.

e) None of the above.

Answer: D

29. When you see a car approaching on your lane you should:

a) Pull to the right and slow down.

b) Sound your horn.

c) At night, flash your lights.

d) All of the above.

e) None of the above.

Answer: D

30. It is legal to park next to a fire hydrant as long as you move your vehicle if necessary.

a) True

b) False

Answer: B

31. In which of the following conditions do you need extra following distance?

a) When driving on slippery roads.

b) When following a motorcycle.

c) When following trucks or vehicles pulling trailers.

d) When it is hard to see.

e) None of the above.

f) All of the above.

Answer: F

32. The Yellow diamond signs with black letters or symbols are what kind of signs?

a) Destination

b) Service

c) Route

d) Reference

e) Regulatory

f) Warning

Answer: F

33. It is very ok to continue at the same speed when an emergency vehicle approaches you with flashing lights and a siren if there is any other lane open.

a) True

b) False

Answer: B

34.   You have to yield to traffic on your left already in the roundabout.

a)   True

b)   False

Answer: A

35.   Which of the following about littering while driving is true?

a)   It may cause a traffic accident.

b)   Is against the law.

c)   It could lead to large fines up to and including jail time.

d)   All of the above.

e)   None of the above.

Answer: D

36.   Which of these influences the effects of alcohol in the body?

a)   How much time between each drink.

b)   The body weight of a person.

c)   The amount of food in the stomach.

d)   All of the above.

e)   None of the above.

Answer: D

37.   Both of these signs shows that you are entering a School

Zone.

a)   True

b)   False

Answer: B

38.   Multiple lanes of travelling in the same direction are separated by lane markings of what color?

a)   Red

b)   Yellow

c)   White

d)   Orange

Answer: C

39. How many drinks would it take to affect your driving?

a) 1

b) 2

c) 3

d) 4

e) 5

Answer: 1

40. What do an orange sign mean?

a) State highway ahead.

b) Merging lanes ahead.

c) Construction work ahead.

d) Divided highway ahead.

e) None of the above.

Answer: C

41. What could be the correct action to take when at a railroad crossing that does not have signals?

a) Come to a complete stop.

b) Slow down and be prepared to stop.

c) Speed to get across the tracks quickly.

d) None of the above.

Answer: B

42. To keep a steady speed and signaling in advance when slowing down or turning will help maintain what

a) A safe distance ahead of your vehicle.

b) A safe distance behind your vehicle.

c) A safe distance next to your vehicle.

d) All of the above.

e) None of the above.

Answer: B

43. Which of the signs below means you are entering a School Zone?

a) A.

b) B.

c)   C.

d)   None of the above.

Answer: D

44.   A solid white line shows what part of the traffic lane on a road?

a)   It separates lanes of traffic moving the opposite directions. Single white lines could also mark the right edge of the pavement.

b)   It separates lanes of traffic moving the same directions. Single white lines could also mark the left edge of the pavement.

c)   It separates lanes of traffic moving the same direction. Single white lines could also mark the right edge of the pavement.

d)   It separates the lanes of traffic moving in the opposite direction. Single white lines may as well mark the left edge of the pavement.

e)   None of the above.

Answer: C

45.   When you make a left turn from a two-way street to a one-way street in which of the lane should your vehicle be in when the turn is completed?

a)   In the right lane.

b) In the left lane.

c) In the center lane.

d) None of the above.

Answer: C

46. Which of these practices is not only dangerous but illegal to do while driving?

a) Adjusting your outside mirrors manually.

b) Wearing headphones that cover both ears.

c) Putting on make-up.

d) Eating and drinking coffee.

e) Reading a map.

Answer: B

47. If a traffic light change from green to yellow as you approach an intersection. What should you do?

a) Keep going at your current speed.

b) Stop before the intersection.

c) Stop, even if in the intersection.

d) Speed up to beat the traffic light before it turns red.

e) None of the above.

Answer: B

48. If you are planning to pull into a driveway immediately after an intersection. When should you signal?

a) After you cross the intersection.

b) Before you cross the intersection.

c) When you start your turn.

d) In the middle of the intersection.

Answer: D

49. What would you do if a railroad crossing has no warning devices?

a) Stop within 15 feet of a railroad crossing.

b) Increase your speed, cross the tracks quickly.

c) Slow down and then proceed with caution.

d) All crossings have a control device.

e) None of the above.

Answer: C

50. What do white painted curbs indicate?

a) Loading zone for freight or passengers.

b) No loading zone.

c) Loading zone for passengers or mail.

d) No loitering.

e) None of the above.

Answer: C

51. Name some places where you may find slippery spots on the road.

a) In corners and at stop signs.

b) In shady spots and on overpasses and bridges.

c) In tunnels and on hills.

d) Near large bodies of water.

e) None of the above.

Answer: B

52. Night driving is very dangerous because?

a) Traffic signs are less visible at night.

b) The distance you see ahead is reduced.

c) People are sleepy at night.

d) Criminals come out at nighttime.

e) None of the above.

Answer: B

53. Which of the following would be most effective in avoiding a collision?

a) Keeping your lights on at all times.

b) Wearing a seat belt.

c) Driving in daytime hours only.

d) Keeping cushion of space at all times.

e) Driving slow at all times

Answer: D

54. What drugs would affect your ability to drive safely?

a) Almost any drug, prescription or over the counter drugs, can affect your ability to drive.

b) Alcohol and marijuana.

c) Only illegal drugs.

d) None of the above.

Answer: A

55. In driving a roundabout, the same general rules apply as for maneuvering through any other type of intersection.

a) True

b) False

Answer: A

56. When a signal light turns green, what would you do?

a) Accelerate as quickly as possible.

b) Yield to pedestrians.

c) Count two seconds before accelerating.

d) Do not move until another driver signals for you to go.

e) None of the above.

Answer: B

57.   At an intersection what should you do with a flashing red light, ?

a)   Come to a stop, then go when safe to do so.

b)   Come to a stop, then go when it flashes green.

c)   Slow down and yield to any vehicle already in the intersection.

d)   Come to a stop, then go when it turns solid green.

Answer: A

58.   When more than one vehicle arrives at the same time at a four way stop, which vehicle should go first?

a)   The first one that attempts to go.

b)   The vehicle on the left.

c)   The vehicle on the right.

d)   None of the above.

Answer: C

59 When can a driver use handicapped parking lot?

a)   If a physically handicapped is in the vehicle when it is parked.

b)   If a handicapped person is being dropped or picked up.

c)   If the vehicle displays a handicapped license plates.

d)   All of the above.

e)   None of the above.

Answer: C

60.   Scanning and seeing events well in advance would help prevent what?

a)   Fatigue

b)   Distractions

c)   Panic stops

d)   Lane changes

e)   None of the above

Answer: C

61.   A white square or a rectangular signs with white, red, or black letters or symbols are usually what kind of signs?

a)   Destination

b)   Service

c)   Route

d)   Reference

e)   Regulatory

f)   Warning

Answer: E

62.   When is it appropriate to obey instructions from school crossing guards?

a)   Only during school hours.

b)   Only if you see children present.

c)   Only if they are licensed crossing guards.

d)   Only at a marked school crosswalk.

e)   At all times.

Answer: E

63.   Which way should you turn your wheels if any, when packing on a downgrade with a curb?

a)   Turn them away from the curb.

b)   Point them straight ahead.

c)   Turn them toward the curb.

d)   Park facing up the hill instead.

e)   None of the above.

Answer: C

64.   Talking on a cell phone while driving may increase your chances of being in a crash by as much as four times.

a)   True

b)   False

Answer: A

65.   When a tire blows out what should you do?

a)   Hold the steering wheel very firmly while easing up on the gas pedal.

b)   Apply the brakes firmly.

c)   Shift to neutral and apply the brakes.

d)   Speed up fast to gain stability, then pull over.

e)   None of the above.

Answer: A

Permit Practice Test 2

(114 Questions)

1.   In your opinion, which of the following is the best example of defensive driving?

a)   Keeping an eye on the car's brake lights in front of you while driving.

b)   Keeping your eyes moving looking for possible hazards.

c)   Putting one car's length between you and the car ahead of you.

d)   Checking your mirrors a couple of times per trip.

Answer: B

2. Driving closely behind a vehicle is known as what?

a) Drafting.

b) Towing.

c) Tailgating.

d) None of the above.

Answer: C

3. When should a driver obey instructions from school crossing guards?

a) Only during school hours.

b) Only if you see children present.

c) Only if they are licensed crossing guards.

d) Only at a marked school crosswalk.

e) At all times.

Answer: E

4. In which of the following situations should horn be used?

a) In which of the following situations should horn be used?

a) To notify a vehicle to move out of the way.

b) To warn bike riders that you are passing.

c) When changing lanes quickly.

d) To prevent a possible accident.

e) To let someone know you are angry.

f) All of the above.

Answer: D5.   Driving and doing any of the following; eating, drinking, angry, ill, and texting are all examples of?

a)   Safe Driving.

b)   Defensive Driving.

c)   Talented Driving.

d)   Distracted Driving.

Answer: D

6.   Keep your eyes on the road, then quickly engage neutral pull off the road when it's safe to do likewise, and turn the engine off. These are things you do when there is?

a)   A tire blowout.

b)   Power failure.

c)   Headlight failure.

d)   A stuck gas pedal.

Answer: D

7.   The cause of most rear end collisions is?

a)   Failing to inspect the vehicle.

b)   Not checking your mirrors.

c)   Talking to passengers.

d)   Following too closely.

Answer: D

8.   Swerving right instead of toward oncoming traffic to prevent a crash is better.

a) True

b) False

Answer: A

9. What do you consider as the correct action to take when at a railroad crossing that does not have signals?

a) Come to a complete stop.

b) Slow down and be prepared to stop.

c) Speed to get across the tracks quickly.

d) None of the above.

Answer: B

10. Which lane would you end up in after completing a turn when turning from one of three turn lanes?

a) The right lane if clear.

b) The lane you started in.

c) The left most lane.

d) Always the middle lane.

Answer: B

11. A cross-buck or white X shaped sign that has Railroad Crossing written on it has the same meaning as a stop sign.

a) True

b) False

Answer: A

12. The moment you have a yellow line on your right and white line on your left are you going the wrong way?

a) Yes

b) No

Answer: A

13. The very minimum amount of a safe following distance is?

a) 2 seconds.

b) 4 seconds.

c) 6 seconds.

d) 8 seconds.

Answer: B

14. A driver turning left at an intersection should yield to which of the following?

a) Vehicles approaching from the opposite direction.

b) Pedestrians, bicycles and vehicles approaching from the opposite direction.

c) Pedestrians, bicycles and vehicles approaching from the right.

d) Pedestrians, bicycles, and vehicles approaching from the left.

e) None of the above.

Answer: B

15. Broken yellow lines separates lanes of traffic going in the same direction

a) True

b) False

Answer: B

16. Except prohibited by a sign, when may one turn left at a red light?

a) In an emergency.

b) From a two way road to a one way road.

c) From a one way road to another one-way road.

d) Never.

Answer: C

17. You may use your horn to alert drivers that they have made an error.

a) True

b) False

Answer: B

18. When exactly is it not legal to turn right at a red light?

a) It is always legal.

b) It is never legal anytime to turn right at a red light.

c) Only on one-way roads.

d) Only if there is a no-turn-on- the red signposted.

Answer: D

19. What would you do if a railroad crossing has no warning devices?

a) Stop at once within 15 feet of the railroad crossing.

b) Increase your speed and cross the tracks very quickly.

c) Slow down and then proceed with caution.

d) All crossings have a control device.

e) None of the above.Answer: C

1. When is it really legal to drive a vehicle in a bicycle lane?

a) When preparing to turn. For less than 200 feet

b) If your hazard lights are on.

c) If there are no bikes.

d) It is never legal to drive a vehicle in a bicycle lane.

Answer: A

2. What does a red painted curb indicate?

a) Loading zone.

b) Reserved for passenger drop off or pick up.

c) No parking or stopping.

Answer: C

3. Which of the following acts is most effective in avoiding a collision?

a) Keeping your lights on at all times.

b) Wearing a seat belt.

c) Driving in daytime hours only.

d) To Keep a cushion of space at all times.

e) Driving slow at all times.

Answer: D

4. Pavement line colors show if you are on a one-way or two-way roadway.

a) True

b)   False

Answer: A

5.   How fast may one drive when driving on a highway posted for 65 mph and the traffic is traveling at 70 mph.

a)   As quickly as the speed of traffic.

b)   Between 65 mph and 70 mph.

c)   As fast as the momentum needed to pass other traffic.

d)   Not faster than 65 mph.

Answer: D

6.   At what point is the road most slippery when raining?

a)   When it first starts to rain.

b)   Only after it has been raining for a while.

c)   After the rain has stopped, but the road is still wet.

d)   None of the above.

Answer: A

7. Keeping your eyes on the road, quickly shifting to neutral, pulling off the road when it is safe to do so, and turning off the engine are the procedures for which of the following ?

a) A stuck gas pedal.

b) A power failure.

c) Brake failure.

d) None of the above.

Answer: A

8. Scanning and seeing events very well in advance will help prevent what?

a) Fatigue

b) Distractions

c) Panic stops

d) Lane changes

Answer: C

9. When do you obey a construction flagger's instructions?

a) Only if you see it is necessary to do so.

b) If they do not conflict with existing signs or signals.

c) If they are wearing a state badge.

d) At all times in construction zones.

e) None of the above.

Answer: D

10. When approaching a road construction work zone, what should you do?

a) Close the distance between your vehicle and any vehicle ahead of you.

b) Prepare to slow down or stop.

c) Prepare to watch the ongoing work.

d) Put on hazard lights to warn other drivers.

Answer: B

11. What do white painted curbs signify?

a) Loading zone for freight or passengers.

b) No loading zone.

c) Loading zone for passengers or mail.

d) No loitering.

e) None of the above.

Answer: C

12. What does an orange sign imply?

a) State highway ahead.

b) Merging lanes ahead.

c) Construction work ahead.

d) Divided highway road ahead.

Answer: C

13. What drug can affect your ability to drive safely?

a) Almost every drug prescription or over the counter drugs can affect your ability to drive.

b) Alcohol and marijuana.

c) Only illegal drugs.

d) None of the above.

Answer: A

14. It is never necessary to signal before you exit a freeway or pull away from a curb?

a) True

b) False

Answer: B

15.   Once you miss your exit on a freeway, it is legal to stop and back up on the shoulder.

a)   True

b)   False

Answer: B

16.   When can one make a left turn at a green light?

a)   Only if there is a green arrow.

b)   Only on a city streets.

c)   Only after yielding to oncoming traffic.

d)   Only on one-way streets.

Answer: C

17.   Which of the following emotions would have a significant effect on your ability to drive safely?

a)   Worried

b)   Excited

c)   Afraid

d) Angry

e) Depressed

f) All of the above

g) None of the above

Answer: F

18. In what situation is it ok to back up on the highway?

a) If you miss your exit.

b) To go back to see an accident.

c) To pick someone on the side of the highway.

d) It is really never ok to back up on the highway.

Answer: D

19. Name some of the places where you are likely to find slippery spots on the road?

a) In corners and at stop signs.

b) shady spots and on overpasses and bridges.

c) In tunnels and on hills.

d) Near large bodies of water.

Answer: B

20.   The best way to enter a freeway very smoothly is to accelerate on the entrance ramp so as to match the speed of freeway traffic in the right lane.

a)   True

b)   False

Answer: A

21.   Which of the these statements about large trucks is true?

a)   Trucks usually travel slower than cars.

b)   Trucks often make wide right turns.

c)   Trucks take longer to stop than cars.

d)   All of the above.

e)   None of the above.

Answer: D

22.   It is legal to park next to a fire hydrant as long as you will move your vehicle if necessary

a)   True

b)   False

Answer: B

23.   Which of the statements below is correct?

a)   A solid or dashed yellow line show the left edge of traffic lanes going in your direction.

b)   Solid or dashed yellow line show the right edge of traffic lanes going in your direction.

Answer: A

24.   When you are driving faster than other traffic on a freeway, which lane should you use?

a)   The right lane.

b)   The shoulder.

c)   The left lane.

d)   The carpool lane.

e)   None of the above.

Answer: C

25.   When you are on the highway, how far ahead should you look?

a)   1 city block.

b)   1 quarter mile.

c)   1 half mile.

d)   1 mile.

Answer: B

26.   What color lines divide lanes of traffic going in opposite directions?

a)   White

b)   Yellow

c)   Orange

d)   Red

Answer: B

27.   If a traffic light turns from green to yellow as you approach an intersection, what should you do?

a)   Stop, even if in the intersection.

b)   Speed up so as to beat the light before it turns red.

c)   Keep going at your current speed.

d)   Stop before the intersection.

Answer: D

28.   When you merge with traffic, at what speed should you try to enter traffic?

a)   A slower speed than traffic.

b)   The same speed as traffic.

c)   A faster speed than traffic.

d)   As fast as you can go.

Answer: B

29.   When you park on an uphill grade, which way should you turn your wheels

a)   Left

b)   Right

c)   Straight

Answer: A

30.   Multiple lanes of travel going in the same direction are usually separated by lane markings of what color?

a)   Red

b) Yellow

c) White

d) Orange

Answer: C

31. How close should one pack when parking next to a curb?

a) Not closer than 6 inches from the curb.

b) Not farther than 6 inches from the curb.

c) Not closer than 12 inches from the curb.

d) Not farther than 18 inches from the curb.

e) Not farther than 24 inches from the curb.

Answer: D

32. What does blind spots mean?

a) Blind spots are places for blind people to cross at an intersection.

b) Blind spots are dots often seen by drivers who have been drinking.

c) Blind spot is an area near the left and right rear corners of your vehicle which you cannot see in your rearview mirrors.

d) Blind spots are spots seen after staring into oncoming headlights at night.

e) None of the above.

Answer: C

33. Signaling in advance and keeping a steady speed when you have to slow down or turn will help maintain what

a) A safe distance ahead of your vehicle.

b) A safe distance behind your vehicle.

c) A safe distance next to your vehicle.

d) All of the above.

Answer: B

34. What is actually the minimum safe following distance under most conditions,?

a) The recommended following distance under most conditions is a minimum of 2 seconds.

b) The minimum of 4 seconds is the recommended following distance in most conditions.

c) It is a minimum of 5 seconds is the recommended following distance in most conditions.

d) It is a minimum of 6 seconds is the recommended following distance under most conditions.

e) None of the above.

Answer: B

35. When is it permissible to drive faster than the posted speed limit?

a) When being followed too closely.

b) To be keeping pace with the flow of traffic.

c) If you have an emergency.

d) It is never ok.

Answer: D

36. One of the basic important things to remember about driving at night or in a fog is to?

a) Be ready to brake more quickly.

b) Watch for cars at intersections.

c) Drive within the range of your headlights.

d) Use your high beams at all times.

e) None of the above.

Answer: C

37.   You must always stop at a minimum of _____ feet from a stopped school bus with its red lights flashing?

a)   10 feet.

b)   20 feet.

c)   30 feet.

d)   50 feet.

Answer: B

38.   One can cross a solid yellow line to do which of the following?

a)   To do a U turn on the highway.

b)   To turn into a driveway only if it is safe to do so.

c)   To pass on the highway.

d)   To get a good view of the road ahead.

Answer: B

39.   When the law enforcement is directing you to drive through a red light, what should you do?

a)   Never ignore traffic signals.

b) Drive through the red light.

c) Wait for the light to turn green.

d) Pull over and stop.

Answer: B

40. When moving at 50 mph it will take approximately how many feet to react to an object on the road and stop your vehicle?

a) 200 feet.

b) 300 feet.

c) 400 feet.

d) 500 feet.

Answer: C

41. You should dim your high beams whenever you come within _____ feet of an oncoming vehicle?

a) 200

b) 300

c) 400

d) 500

Answer: D

42.   A cross-buck or white X shaped sign that says Railroad Crossing on it has the same meaning as a yield sign

a)   True

b)   False

Answer: A

43.   Night driving is said to be more dangerous because?

a)   Traffic signs are less visible at night.

b)   The distance one can see ahead is reduced.

c)   People are sleepy at night.

d)   Criminals come out at nighttime.

e)   None of the above.

Answer: B

44.   What do a yellow sign mean?

a)   State highway ahead.

b)   A special situation or a hazard ahead.

c)   Construction work ahead.

d)   Interstate sign.

45.   When driving at a roundabout, the same general rules apply as for maneuvering through any other type of intersection

a)   True

b)   False

46.   A solid white line signifies what part of the traffic lane on a road?

a)   It separates the lanes of traffic moving in opposite directions. Single white lines can also mark the right edge of the pavement.

b)   It separates lanes of traffic moving in same direction. Single white lines may also mark the left edge of the pavement.

c)   It separates lanes of traffic moving the same direction. Single white lines can also mark the right edge of the pavement.

d It separates lanes of traffic moving the opposite way. Single white lines can also mark the left edge of the pavement.

e)   None of the above.

Answer: C

47. While driving a motor vehicle, both hands should be on the steering wheel at all times except you are texting.

a) True

b) False

Answer: B

48. If more than one vehicle is stopped at an intersection, which vehicle has the right-of-way

a) The largest vehicle.

b) The first vehicle that attempts to go.

c) The first vehicle to arrive.

d) The vehicle on the right.

e) None of the above.

Answer: C

49. If ever a tire blows out, you should?

a) Hold the steering wheel very firmly while easing up on the gas pedal.

b) Apply the brakes firmly.

c)   Shift to neutral and apply the brakes.

d)   Speed up to gain stability, and pull over.

e)   None of the above.

Answer: A

50.   In which of these conditions would you need an extra following distance

a)   When driving on slippery roads.

b)   When following a motorcycle.

c)   When following trucks or vehicles pulling trailers.

d)   When it is hard to see.

e)   None of the above.

f)   All of the above.

Answer:

51.   Whenever you want to turn left at an intersection but oncoming traffic is heavy. What should you do

a)   Wait at the crosswalk for traffic to clear.

b)   Wait right in the center of the intersection for traffic to clear.

c)   Start your turn forcing others to stop.

d)   None of the above.

Answer: B

52.   A motorist when approaching a bicyclist should?

a)   Hurry and pass him.

b)   Proceed as normal.

c)   Swerve into the opposite lane.

d)   Exercise extreme caution.

e)   Stay behind following at a safe distance

Answer: D

53.   Talking on cell phone may increase your chances of being in a crash by as much as four times.

a)   True

b)   False

Answer: A

54.   Driving relatively much slower than the speed limit in normal conditions can do what?

a) It can decrease the chance of an accident.

b) It does not change anything.

c) It can increase driver safety.

d) It can increase the chances of an accident.

Answer: D

55.   Any pedestrian using a white or a red-tipped white cane is usually what?

a)   A policeman.

b)   A construction worker.

c)   A blind person.

d)   A crossing guard.

e)   None of the above.

Answer: C

56.   Trying to move too fast from a stop could cause which of the following?

a)   Battery strain.

b)   Stuck gas pedal.

c)   Spinning drive wheels.

d)   Excessive smiling.

e)   None of the above.

Answer: C

57.   What type of vehicles must stop at all railroad crossings?

a)   All vehicles.

b)   Recreational vehicles.

c)   School buses and passenger buses.

d)   18 wheelers.

e)   All of the above.

Answer: C

58.   What is really the correct left-turn hand signal?

a)   Hand and arm extended downward.

b)   Hand and arm extended out.

c)   Hand and arm extended upward.

d) Hand and arm is extended upward with middle finger extended upward

Answer: B

59. Which of these practices is not only dangerous but illegal to do while driving?

a) Adjusting your outside mirrors manually.

b) Wearing headphones that cover both ears.

c) Putting on make-up.

d) Eating and drinking coffee.

e) Reading a map

Answer: B

60. Whenever you park uphill on a street with no curb, which way should your front wheels be turned?

a) To the left.

b) To the right.

c) Parallel with the road.

d) None of the above

Answer: B

61. When driving in the snow or rain during the day you should?

a) Use your high beams.

b) Use your fog lights.

c) Use your low beams.

d) Use no headlights.

Answer: D

62. During a skid, one should steer to the left if the rear of the vehicle is skidding in what direction?

a) The left.

b) The right.

Answer: A

63. While waiting at the intersection to complete a left turn, you should

a) Blow your horn so vehicles will let you get through.

b) Signal and wait for an opening while you keep your wheels turned to the left.

c) Signal and wait for an opening while you keep your wheels turned straight.

d)   Put on your headlights.

Answer: C

64.   The most important thing to always remember when controlling a skid is to apply the brakes firmly

a)   True

b)   False

Answer: B

65.   Passing on the right is permissible when it is safe and the driver of the other vehicle is making a left turn

a)   True

b)   False

Answer: A

66.   You are not required to make a full stop in which situation?

a)   At a steady red traffic signal.

b)   At a flashing yellow traffic signal.

c)   At a stop sign.

d)   At a flashing red traffic signal.

Answer: B

67. How many drinks could it take to affect your driving

a) 1

b) 2

c) 3

d) 4

e) 5

Answer: A

68. Motorcycles cannot stop as quickly as anyother vehicle can?

a) True

b) False

Answer: A

69. When turning left from a two-way street to a one way street, your vehicle should be in which lane when the turn is completed

a) In the right lane.

b) In the left lane.

c) In the center lane.

d) None of the above.

Answer: B

70. You are never to pass on the right if it means driving off the paved or main portion of the roadway

a) True

b) False

Answer: B

71. How many feet should you signal before your intended turn?

a) 25 feet.

b) 50 feet.

c) 75 feet.

d) 100 feet.

e) 200 feet.

Answer: D

72. It's ok to pass when approaching a hill-top or a curve if you hurry?

a) True

b) False

Answer: B

73. How can you see when there is a car in your blind spot?

a) Lean backward and forth looking in your mirrors.

b) Look over your shoulder.

c) Adjust the power mirrors if you have them.

d) Nothing can be done, that is why it is called a blind spot.

Answer:: B

74. When you are on the highway, how far ahead should you look?

a) 3 to 5 seconds.

b) 5 to 10 seconds.

c) 10 to 15 seconds.

d) 15 to 20 seconds.

Answer:C

75. If you are on the highway entrance and have to wait for a gap in traffic before entering the roadway, what should you do?

a) Pull up on the ramp as far as you can and wait leaving some room behind you on the ramp for other vehicles.

b) Drive quickly to the shoulder and wait for a gap in the roadway, then accelerate quickly.

c) Slow down on the entrance ramp and wait for a gap, then speed up so you enter at the same speed that traffic the is moving.

d) Slow down on the entrance ramp and wait for a gap, then sound the horn and also activate your emergency flashing lights to alert drivers that you are entering the roadway.

Answer: C

a) How far ahead should look when you are driving in town?

a. 1 city block.

b. 1 quarter mile.

c. 1 half mile.

d. 1 mile.

Answer: A

76. When you experience glare from a vehicles headlights at night you should?

a) Look above their headlights.

b) Look below their headlights.

c) Be Looking towards the right edge of your lane.

d) Be Looking toward the left edge of your lane.

Answer: C

77. Whenever you pass a vehicle traveling in the same direction, you are expected to pass on the left?

a) True

b) False

Answer: A

78. What do broken white line on the highway signify?

a) A broken white lines separates two lanes traveling in opposite directions. Once you have signaled and it is safe to do so, you may cross this line when changing lanes.

b) A broken white line separates two lanes that travels the same direction. Do not cross this line.

c) A broken white line separates is two lanes traveling the opposite direction. Do not cross this line.

d)   A broken white line is often used to separate two lanes traveling the same direction. Once you have signaled and it is safe to do so, you may cross this line when changing lanes.

e)   None of the above.

Answer: A

79.   If you have entered an intersection already when the light changes, you should?

a)   Stop in the intersection.

b)   Proceed and clear the intersection.

c)   Flash your lights through the intersection.

d)   Sound your horn through the intersection.

Answer: B

80.   To pass a vehicle stopped for pedestrians in a crosswalk is legal

a)   True

b)   False

Answer: A

81. To pass on the right is permissible though not ideal on a one-way road, streets and highways that are marked for two or more lanes of traffic moving in the same direction.

a) True

b) False

Answer: A

82. You have to give-in to traffic on your right already in a roundabout.

a) True

b) False

Answer: B

83. Whenever you drive in a heavy fog during the daytime you should drive with your

a) Headlights off.

b) Parking lights on.

c) Headlights on low beam.

d) Headlights on high beam.

e) None of the above.

Answer: C

84.   Hitting any vehicle moving in the opposite direction is better than hitting one moving in the same direction

a)   True

b)   False

Answer: B

85.   You could cross a double yellow line to pass another vehicle if the yellow line next to you is what

a)   A solid line.

b)   A thinner line.

c)   A broken line.

d)   A thicker line.

e)   None of the above.

Answer: C

86.   If you have a green light, and traffic is backed up into the intersection, what should you do?

a)   Enter the intersection and hope that traffic clears before the light changes.

b)   Wait for traffic to clear before you enter the intersection.

c)   Try to go around the traffic.

d)   Sound your horn to clear the intersection

Answer: B

87.   There are some circumstance where it is legal to double park

a)   True

b)   False

Answer: B

88.   Which lane should you be in if you are traveling 47 mph on a highway with a speed limit of 55 mph?

a)   The far left lane.

b)   The carpool lane.

c)   The far right lane.

d)   The middle lane.

e)   The bicycle lane.

Answer: C

89.   Which vehicle goes first if more than one vehicle arrives at the same time at a four way stop?

a)   The first one that attempts to go.

b)   The vehicle on the left.

c)   The vehicle on the right.

d)   None of the above.

Answer: C

90.   What would you do at an intersection with a flashing red light?

a)   Come to a full stop, and go whenever it flashes green.

b)   Come to a full stop, and go whenever it is safe to do so.

c)   Slow down and yield to any vehicle already in the intersection.

d)   Come to a full stop, then go whenever it turns solid green

Answer: B

91.   When should safety belts be worn?

a)   At all times while driving and as a passenger.

b)   Only when driving on curvy roads.

c)   Only when riding in the back seat.

d)   Only when driving on the freeway.

e)   None of the above.

Answer: A

92.   When approaching any intersection with traffic control signals that are not working, you should treat it as you would a 4-way yield sign

a)   True

b)   False

Answer: B

93.   What does a flashing yellow light indicate?

a)   Stop, then proceed with caution.

b)   Proceed with caution.

c)   Pedestrian crossing.

d)   School Crossing.

e)   None of the above.

Answer: B

94. Which one of these does not affect braking distance?

a) Turn them away from the curb.

b) Point them straight ahead.

c) Turn them toward the curb.

d) Park facing up the hill instead.

e) None of the above

Answer: C

95. What would you do if you are at an intersection and you hear a siren

a) Stop and do not move until every emergency vehicle has passed.

b) Continue through the intersection, and pull over to the right side of the road and stop.

c) Back up then, pull over to the right side of the road and stop.

d) None of the above

Answer: B

96. If any driver is following you too closely you should?

a) Slowly speed up.

b) Jam the brakes.

c) Flash your brake lights 3 times.

d) Move over to another lane when there is room.

e) None of the above.

Answer: D

97.   After drinking, a cold shower or coffee will lower your blood alcohol content.

a)   True

b)   False

Answer: B

98.   Whenever an emergency vehicle is approaching you with a siren and flashing lights it is ok to continue at the same speed if there is another lane open.

a)   True

b)   False

Answer: B

99. Whenever you see a stopped vehicle on the side of the road what would you do?

a) Stop and offer assistance.

b) Slow down and use caution when passing.

c) Sound the horn to let them know that you are about to pass them.

d) Notify emergency services.

e) None of the above.

Answer: B

100. Quickly tapping the brake pedal 3 or 4 times would help to let those driving behind you know that you are about slowing down.

a) True

b) False

Answer: A

101. When passing, you may exceed the posted speed limit only when passing a group of cars.

a) True

b) False

Answer: F

102. Which of the following influences the effects of alcohol in the body

a) How much time there is between each drink.

b) The body weight of a person.

c) The amount of food in the stomach.

d) All of the above.

e) None of the above.

Answer: D

103. Whenever you drive on slippery roads, you should increase your following distance by _____

a) 2 times.

b) 3 times.

c) 4 times.

d) 5 times.

Answer: A

104. You must use high beam lighting during heavy rain, in fog, and snow.

a) True

b) False

Answer: A

105. Passing is permissible in either direction when there are two solid yellow lines in the center of the road when?

a) When following a slow truck.

b) Only whenever you are sure it is safe.

c) On US highways only.

d) Passing is never permitted

Answer: D

106. During a heavy rain, you can lose all traction and start hydroplaning at?

a) 25 mph

b) 40 mph

c) 50 mph

d) 65 mph

Answer: C

107. Safety belts would help you keep control of your car?

a) True

b) False

Answer: A

108. On a rainy, foggy, or snowy day when it starts to get dark, and if driving off a rising or setting sun, it is a very good time to?

a) Check the tires.

b) Put on your seatbelt.

c) Turn on your headlights.

d) Roll up the windows.

Answer: C

109. If your vehicle suddenly begins to skid you should?

a) Use the brake, and turn the steering wheel in the direction that you desire the vehicle to go.

b) Avoid the brake and turn the steering wheel in the direction that you want the vehicle to go.

c) Use the brake and turn the steering wheel in the direction that you do not want the vehicle to go.

d) Avoid the brake and turn the steering wheel in the direction you do not want the vehicle to go.

Answer: B

110. When could you signal if you plan to pull into a driveway just after an intersection?

a) After you cross the intersection.

b) Before you cross the intersection.

c) When you start your turn.

d) In the middle of the intersection.

Answer: A

111. You may turn your vehicle while braking with ABS with less or no skidding than with regular brakes.

a) True

b) False

Answer: A

112. In which of these places must you never park

a) On sidewalks.

b) In bicycle lanes.

c) In front of driveways.

d) By fire hydrants.

e) All of the above.

Answer: E

113. When may you legally block an intersection?

a) During rush hour traffic.

b) If you entered an intersection when the light was green light.

c) You cannot legally block an intersection.

d) When the light is yellow.

e) None of the above.

Answer: E

114. Where are ramp meters usually located?

a) In parking garages.

b) On Loading docks.

c) On highway exit ramps.

d) On highway entrance ramps.

e) None of the above.

Answer: C

Practice Test 3

(54 Questions)

1. Which of these places should you never park?

a) On sidewalks.

b) In bicycle lanes.

c) In front of driveways.

d) By fire hydrants.

e) All of the above.

Answer: E

2. What does this hand signal signify?

a) Left turn.

b) Right turn.

c) Stop or slowing down.

d) Backing.

e) None of the above.

Answer: B

3. If driving in the rain or snow during the day you should?

a) Use your high beams.

b) Use your fog lights.

c) Use your low beams.

d) Use no headlights.

Answer: B

4. Hitting any vehicle moving in the opposite direction is more better than hitting a vehicle moving in the same direction.

a) True

b) False

Answer: B

5. If you have entered an intersection already when the light changes, you should?

a) Stop in the intersection.

b) Proceed and clear the intersection.

c) Flash your lights through the intersection.

d) Sound your horn through the intersection.

Answer: B

6. What do blind spots mean?

a) Blind spots are places for blind people to cross at an intersection.

b) Blind spots are dots often seen by drivers who have been drinking.

c) Blind spots are those areas near the left and right rear corners of the vehicle that you cannot see in your rearview mirrors.

d)   Blind spots are spots seen after staring into oncoming headlights at night.

e)   None of the above.

Answer: C

7.   If really you hurry it is ok to pass when you approach the top of a hill or a curve.

a)   True

b)   False

Answer: B

8.   Driving very much slower than the speed limit in normal conditions may do what?

a)   It can decrease the chance of an accident.

b)   It does not change anything.

c)   It can increase driver safety.

d)   It can really increase the chance of an accident.

Answer: D

9.   It is a must that you use high beam lighting in fog, snow, and heavy rain.

a) True

b) False

Answer: B

10. You must avoid passing on the right if it means driving off the paved or main portion of the roadway.

a) True

b) False

Answer: A

11. If a driver is approaching an intersection, with the traffic light showing green and the driver wants to drive straight through. While another vehicle is already in the intersection making a left turn. Who has the right-of-way?

a) The driver who wants to drive straight.

b) The driver who is turning left.

Answer: B

12. A cross-buck sign or a white X shaped that says Railroad Crossing on it has the same meaning as a stop sign.

a) True

b) False

Answer: B

13. Whenever you pass a vehicle traveling in the same direction, you should pass on the left.

a) True

b) False

Answer: A

14. Which lane will you end up in after completing your turn, when turning from one of three turn lanes?

a) The right lane if clear.

b) The lane you started in.

c) The left most lane.

d) Always the middle lane.

Answer: B

15. If you are traveling at 47 mph on a highway with a speed limit of 55 mph, which lane should you be in?

a) The far left lane.

b) The carpool lane.

c)   The far right lane.

d)   The middle lane.

e)   The bicycle lane.

Answer: C

16.   A pedestrian that uses a white or a red-tipped white cane is usually what?

a)   A policeman.

b)   A construction worker.

c)   A blind person.

d)   A crossing guard.

Answer: C

17.   Traffic Light Meaning: The light usually changes from green to red. Be prepared to always stop for the red light.

a)   Red arrow.

b)   Steady yellow.

c)   Flashing yellow.

d)   Green arrow.

e) Steady green.

f) None of the above.

Answer: B

18. When you experience glare from a vehicles headlights at night you should?

a) Look above their headlights.

b) Look below their headlights.

c) Look towards the right- edge of your lane.

d) Look toward the left- edge of your lane.

Answer: C

19. What does a red painted curb indicate?

a) Loading zone.

b) Reserved only for passenger pick up or drop off.

c) No parking or stopping.

Answer: C

20. What do you think this hand signal mean?

a) Left Turn.

b) Right Turn.

c) Stop or Slowing Down.

d) Backing.

e) None of the above.

Answer: A

21.   You can cross double yellow line to pass another vehicle if only the yellow line next to you is what?

a) A solid line.

b) A thinner line.

c) A broken line.

d) A thicker line.

e) None of the above.

Answer: C

22.   After being pulled over by the law enforcement, you should immediately exit the vehicle and quickly approach the officer's police car.

a)   True

b)   False

Answer: B

23.   Traffic Light Meaning: Stop, yield to the right-of-way, and go when it is safe.

a)   Red arrow.

b)   Steady yellow.

c)   Flashing yellow.

d)   Green arrow.

e)   Flashing red.

f)   None of the above.

Answer: E

24.   What is the minimum safe-following distance under most conditions?

a)   A minimum of 2 seconds is the most recommended following distance under most conditions.

b)   A minimum of 4 seconds is the most recommended following distance under most conditions.

c)   A minimum of 5 seconds is the most recommended following distance under most conditions.

d)   A minimum of 6 seconds is the most recommended following distance under most conditions.

e)   An unbalanced load with much weight on any one axle.

f)   None of the above.

Answer: B

25.   It is not necessary to signal before pulling away from a curb or exits a freeway.

a)   True

b)   False

Answer: A

26.   Eating, drinking, angry, ill, and texting while driving are all examples of?

a)   Safe Driving

b) Defensive Driving

c) Talented Driving

d) Distracted driving

Answer: D

27. It will be better to swerve right instead of toward oncoming traffic to prevent a crash.

a) True

b) False

Answer: A

28. A Pentagon shaped sign signify which of the following?

a) No Passing Zone.

b) Railroad Crossing.

c) School Zone.

d) Yield.

e) Stop.

Answer: C

29.   Unless prohibited by a sign, when can one turn left at a red light?

a)   In an emergency.

b)   From a two way road to a one way road.

c)   From a one-way road to a one way road.

d)   Never.

Answer: C

30.   Keep your eyes always on the road, quickly shift to neutral, pull off the road when it is really safe to do so, then turn off the engine are the procedures for which of the following?

a)   A stuck gas pedal.

b)   A power failure.

c)   Brake failure.

d)   None of the above.

Answer: A

31.   You should always avoid placing infants or a small child in the front seat of a vehicle with airbags.

a)   True

b) False

Answer: A

32. Passing on the right is really permitted only when it is safe and the other vehicle's driveer is making a left turn.

a) True

b) False

Answer: A

33. When you drive on slippery roads, you should increase your following distance by _____.

a) 2 times.

b) 3 times.

c) 4 times.

d) 5 times.

Answer: A

34. While operating a motor vehicle, your both hands should be on the steering wheel at all times except you are texting

a) True

b) False

Answer: B

35.   If driving on a highway posted for 65 mph and the traffic is traveling at 70 mph, how fast would you legally drive?

a)   As fast as the speed of traffic.

b)   Between 65 mph and 70 mph.

c)   As fast as the necessary speed needed to pass other traffic.

d)   No faster than 65 mph.

Answer: D

36.   In which of these situations is it ok to back up on the highway?

a)   If you miss your exit.

b)   To go back to see an accident.

c)   To pick up somebody on the side of the highway.

d)   It is never really ok to back up on the highway.

Answer: D

37.   A driver who approaches an intersection should yield the right-of-way to traffic that is at the intersection.

a)   True

b)   False

Answer: A

38.   When you are on the highway how far ahead should you look?

a)   A block away.

b)   A quarter mile

c)   A half mile

d)   A full mile

Answer: B

39.   Most rear-end collisions are caused by vehicle's at the back following too closely.

a)   True

b)   False

Answer: A

40. When should you realy obey a construction flagger's instructions?

a) Only if you see it is necessary to do so.

b) If they do not conflict with existing signs or signals.

c) If they are wearing a state badge.

d) At all times in construction zones.

e) None of the above.

Answer: D

41. When another driver follows you too closely you should?

a) Slowly speed up.

b) Jam the brakes.

c) Flash your brake lights 3 times.

d) Move to any other lane if there is room.

e) None of the above.

Answer: D

42. The picture below represents the improper hand placement on the steering wheel.

a) True

b) False

Answer: A

43. Keeping your eyes always locked straight ahead is a good defensive driving practice.

a) True

b) False

Answer: B

44. Broken yellow lines is used to separate lanes of traffic going the same direction.

a) True

b) False

Answer: B

45. When exactly should safety belts be worn?

a) At all times as a passenger and as driver.

b) Only when driving on curvy roads.

c) Only when riding in the back seat.

d) Only when driving on the freeway.

e) None of the above.

Answer: A

46. When you park on an uphill grade, which way should you turn your wheels?

a) Left

b) Right

c) Straight

d) None of the above

Answer: A

47. The best way to enter a freeway smoothly is to accelerate on the entrance ramp to match the speed of freeway traffic on the right lane.

a) True

b) False

Answer: A

48.   Pavement line colors would indicate if you are on a one-way or two-way roadway.

a)   True

b)   False

Answer: A

49.   What does this hand signal indicate?

a)   Left turn.

b)   Right turn.

c)   Stop or slowing down.

d)   Backing.

e)   None of the above.

Answer: C

50.   Traffic Light Meaning: You must not go in the direction of the arrow until the light is off and a green arrow or a green light comes on.

a)   Red arrow.

b)   Steady yellow.

c)   Flashing yellow.

d)   Green arrow.

e)   Steady green.

f)   None of the above.

Answer: A

51.   When you parking next to a curb, how close should you park when?

a)   Not closer than 6 inches from the curb.

b)   Not farther than 6 inches from the curb.

c)   Not closer than 12 inches from the curb.

d)   Not any farther than 18 inches from the curb.

e)   Not farther than 24 inches from the curb.

Answer: D

52.   Whenever you approach an intersection with traffic control signals that are not working, you must treat it as you would a 4-way yield-sign.

a)   True

b)   False

Answer: A

53.   Which of these is a very good example of defensive driving?

a)   Keeping an eye on the car's brake lights in front of you while driving.

b)   Keeping your eyes moving to look-out for possible hazards.

c)   Putting a car's length between you and the car ahead of you.

d)   Checking your mirrors a couple times per trip.

Answer: B

54.   How far ahead should you be looking when you are driving in town?

a)   1 city block.

b)   1 quarter mile.

c)   1 half mile.

d)   1 mile.

Answer: A

Practice Test 4

(11 Questions)

1.   Which of the following emotions would have a great effect on your ability to drive safely?

a)   Worried

b)   Excited

c)   Afraid

d)   Angry

e)   Depressed

f)   All of the above

g)   None of the above

Answer: F

2.   Though, both your judgment and vision are affected after drinking alcohol. Which is affected first?

a)   Judgment

b) Vision

Answer: A

3. What color of lines divide lanes of traffic going in opposite directions?

a) White

b) Yellow

c) Orange

d) Red

e) None of the above.

Answer: B

4. Is the vehicle above performing a legal pass?

a) Yes

b) No

Answer: B

5. In which of these situations should one use horn?

a) To notify a vehicle to get out of your way.

b) To warning bike riders that you are passing.

c) When changing lanes quickly.

d) To prevent a possible accident.

e) To let someone know you are angry.

f) All of the above.

Answer: D

6. Below is the proper hand-placement on a steering wheel.

a) True

b) False

Answer: B

7. A full 24 hours of being awake really causes impairment that is nearly equal to that of an alcohol content of what?

a) .02

b) .05

c) .08

d) .10

Answer: D

8. Whenever you see a vehicle coming toward you in your lane you should turn to the left.

a) True

b) False

Answer: B

9. When you merge with traffic, at what speed should you try to enter traffic?

a) A slower speed than traffic.

b) The same speed as traffic.

c) A faster speed than traffic.

d) As fast as you can go.

e) None of the above.

Answer: B

10. Can you ever be issued a ticket for driving too slowly?

a) True

b) False

Answer: A

11. Besides helping you see at night, headlights help other road users see you at any time.

a) True

b) False

Answer: A

Drivers Road Sign

(46 Questions)

A   B   C

1. Put these signs above in proper order from left to right.

a) Guide, warning, stop.

b) Regulatory, service, stop.

c) Regulatory, guide, stop.

d) Warning, service, stop.

e) Warning, guide, stop.

Answer: E

A   B   C

2. Which of the sign above is not a route sign?

a) A.

b) B.

c) C.

d) None of the above.

Answer: C

3. What does this sign mean?

a) Go, yield or stop

b) Yield

c) Stop ahead

d) Signal ahead

e) Caution, no signal at crossing

Answer: D

4. This traffic sign informs you of what?

a) Eat if you are hungry.

b) No silverware beyond this point.

c) Food available at the next exit.

d) his is just highway art.

Answer: C

5. What kind of sign is this?

a) Warning sign.

b) Regulatory sign.

c) Construction sign.

d) Guide sign.

e) None of the above.

Answer: B

6. Yellow sign with black lettering like the one above is called regulatory signs.

a. True

b. False

Answer: B

7. Sign B is a speed limit sign

a) True

b) False

Answer: B

8. What does this sign mean?

a) Look to your right.

b) Stop if turning right.

c) Curve to the right.

d) Sharp turn to the right.

e) None of the above

Answer: C

9. Put the signs above in proper order from left to right.

a) Construction, school crossing, yield.

b) Pedestrian crossing, construction, no passing.

c) School crossing, construction, yield.

d) School crossing, construction, no passing.

e) Pedestrian crossing, construction, yield.

Answer: D

10. What does this sign mean

a) Construction worker.

b) Pedestrian crossing.

c) School crossing.

d) Jogging path.

e) None of the above.

Answer: C

11. In your opinion what really is the meaning of the above sign?

a) This is not a real sign.

b) Pass with care.

c) Uneven shoulder ahead.

d) Narrow bridge ahead.

e) None of the above.

Answer: D

12. Which of these options best describes this sign?

a) Road splits

b) Yield

c) Merge

d) Divided highway

e) Right lane ends

Answer: C

13. What does this bicycle sign mean?

a) Bicycles race starts here.

b) No bicycles.

c) Bicycle crossing.

d) Bicycles must park by the arrow.

e) None of the above.

Answer: C

A   B   C

14.   Sign A above is the state highway sign

a)   True

b)   False

Answer: A

15.   This sign means which of the following

a)   Road splits

b)   Yield

c)   Merge

d)   Divided highway

e)   Right lane ends

Answer: E

16. Put the signs above in their proper order from left to right?

a) Slow moving vehicle, yield, school zone.

b) Yield, no passing, slow moving vehicle.

c) No passing, slow moving vehicle, yield.

d) School crossing, construction, yield.

e) Pedestrian crossing, slow moving vehicle, yield.

Answer: C

17. Which sign above means two-way-traffic?

a) A.

b) B.

c) C.

d) None of the above.

Answer: C

18. All 3 signs above mean yield

a) True

b) False

Answer: A

19. What kind of a signs is square or rectangular signs with blue and white letters or symbols?

a) Destination

b) Service

c) Route

d)   Reference

e)   Regulatory

f)   Warning

Answer: B

20.   Which of the sign above is found on the back of a slow moving vehicle?

a)   A.

b)   B.

c)   C.

d)   None of the above.

Answer: B

21.   Which sign above is a construction sign?

a)   A.

b)   B.

c)   C.

d)   None of the above.

Answer:D

22.   This sign warns that you should

a)   Hurry and pass someone.

b)   Pass only in an emergency.

c)   Never pass.

d)   Pass on the left.

e)   None of the above.

Answer: C

23.   This sign means which of the following?

a)   Look to your left.

b)   Stop if turning left.

c)   Curve to the left.

d)   Sharp turn to the left.

e)   None of the above.

Answer: D

24.   does this sign mean?

a)   4 way stop ahead.

b)   An intersection of roads ahead.

c) Divided roadway.

d) Yield ahead.

e) None of the above.

Answer: B

25.   Which sign above means do not enter?

a)   A.

b)   B.

c)   C.

d)   None of the above.

Answer: B

26.   Which of the above signs mean a divided highway?

a)   A.

b)   B.

c) C.

d) None of the above.

Answer: A

27. It is ok to go 5 mph above most speed limit signs

a) True

b) False

Answer: B

28. What does this sign mean

a) No turning while the light is red even if the road is clear.

b) No turning on green or red.

c) You must ensure the road is clear and if the light is red, then you can turn.

d) None of the above.

Answer: A

29. What is the meaning of this sign?

a) Burning building ahead.

b) Firetruck could be entering the road ahead.

c) Truck blocking the road.

d) No trucks ahead.

e) None of the above.

Answer: B

30. This sign means which of the following

a) Runaway trucks.

b) Hill.

c) Truck parked on right triangle ahead.

d) Truck crossing.

e) None of the above.

Answer: B

31. Which sign above means passing permitted

a) A.

b) B.

c) C.

d) None of the above.

Answer: D

32. Which of these best describes this signs meaning?

a) Construction worker.

b) Pedestrian crossing.

c) School crossing.

d) Jogging path.

e) None of the above.

Answer: B

33. This sign means which of the following?

a) Look both ways.

b) Entering 2 way traffic ahead.

c) You can go forward or reverse.

d) One way traffic.

e) None of the above.

Answer: B

34. This sign means which of the following?

a) Multiple curves ahead.

b) Oil on the road.

c) Slippery when wet.

d) Pavement ends.

e) No drunk drivers.

Answer: C

35. This sign means which of the following

a) Stop.

b) Stop if going straight.

c) Stop ahead.

d) No stop if proceeding straight.

e) None of the above.

Answer: C

36. What color lettering is found on Sign A above

a) Red.

b) Black.

c) White.

d) Yellow.

e) None of the above.

Answer: C

A   B   C

37. Which of the above sign is found on the back of a slow moving vehicle?

a) A.

b) B.

c) C.

d) None of the above.

Answer: D

38. This is a real traffic sign

a) True

b) False

Answer: A

39. Which sign above means no passing is permitted

a) A.

b) B.

c) C.

d) None of the above.

Answer: C

40. Which of the sign above is not a guide sign?

a) A.

b) B.

c) C.

d)   B and C.

e)   A and C.

f)   None of the above.

Answer: D

41.   The sign above shares the same meaning with a _____ sign

a)   Stop.

b)   Yield.

c)   Merge.

d)   Stop ahead.

e)   None of the above.

Answer: B

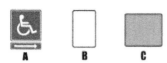

A   B   C

42. Which of the signs above is a warning sign

a) A.

b) B.

c) C.

d) None of the above.

Answer: D

43. What does this orange sign mean?

a) One handed man with lunch.

b) Beware of car jacking.

c) Construction flagger ahead.

d) Watch for pedestrians.

e) None of the above.

Answer: C

A   B   C

44.   Which sign above is a guide sign?

a)   A.

b)   B.

c)   C.

d)   None of the above.

Answer: C

45.   Which of these best describes this sign's meaning?

a)   Road spins.

b)   Drive in circles.

c)   Roundabout ahead.

d)   Circular highway.

e) None of the above.

Answer: C

46. What does this sign mean?

a) Road splits

b) Yield

c) Merge

d) Divided highway

e) Right lane ends

Answer: D

TEEN DRIVER SAFETY

(14 Questions)

1. What is the leading cause of death for teens in the US?

a) Cancer

b) Suicide

c) Auto crashes

d) Murder

Answer: C

2. Teenagers that are between the ages of 16 to 19 are __ times more likely than drivers 20 and over to be in a fatal crash

a) 0

b) 2

c) 3

d) 4

Answer: C

3. 16 to 17 year old driver fatality rates decrease with each additional passenger added to a vehicle.

a) True

b) False

Answer: B

4. 63 percent of teenage passenger deaths in 2008 occurred in vehicles driven by another teenager.

a) True

b) False

Answer: A

5. How many high school teens drank alcohol and drove in 2011?

a) 1,000 teens.

b) 10,000 teens.

c) 100,000 teens.

d) 1,000,000 teens

Answer: D

6. 55 percent of teen driving deaths occur on which days?

a) Monday and Tuesday

b) Wednesdays

c) Thursdays

d) Friday, Saturday, and Sunday

Answer: D

7. The vehicle death rate for teen male drivers and passengers is almost twice that of females.

a) True

b) False

Answer: A

8. Which age group is 3 times more likely to die in a motor vehicle crash than the average of all other drivers combined?

a) 16

b) 17

c) 18

d) 19

Answer: A

9. The risk of vehicle crash are higher for which age group over all other groups?

a) 16 to 19

b) 20 to 22

c) 23 to 25

d) Age does not matter

Answer: A

10. 22 percent of drivers between the age of 15 and 20 involved in fatal crashes were drinking in 2010

a) True

b) False

Answer: A

11. Teens have the lowest rate of using seat belt compared with other age groups.

a) True

b) False

Answer: A

12. Will you share this quiz with a teen you care about?

a) Yes

b) No

Answer: A

13. Two hundred and eighty two thousand teens were injured in vehicle crashes in 2010

a) True

b) False

Answer: A

14. What percent of teenage motor vehicle crash deaths in 2008 were passengers in the vehicles?

a) 22

b) 37

c) 56

d) 81

Answer: D

New Driving Laws Effective since January 1, 2018

It is illegal to ingest or smoke marijuana or any marijuana product while driving a motor vehicle on a highway or while riding as a passenger in a motor vehicle that is being driven on the highways.

Motorcycle Training Course

An Applicant that is 21 years old or older will now have more motorcycle training program options.

Buses and Seat-belts

Effective from July 1, 2018, it is required that a passenger in a bus equipped with seat belts must be really
restrained by a seat-belt, except as specified. Parents, legal

guardians, or chartering parties are now prohibited from transporting on a bus, or permitting to be transported on a bus, any child who is at least 8 years old but still under 16 years old, unless they are properly restrained by a safety belt.

The New DMV which has been effective from April 2018, DMV has began to offer an online driver's license and identification application process. Applicants now have the opportunity to commence their electronic application even before visiting DMV. Be sure to bring the application confirmation with you while to your office visit.

Made in the USA
Monee, IL
18 October 2021